The Easter Story

Bible Activity Book

Compiled by Karen Rhodes

Layout by Christian Elden

The purchase of this coloring book grants you the rights to photocopy the contents for classroom use.
Notice: It is unlawful to copy these pages for resale purposes.
Copy permission is for private use only.

Copyright © 2014 Warner Press, Inc. All rights reserved. Made in USA

Warner Press Kids
educate • nurture • inspire
www.warnerpress.org

30580029517

Long ago God sent His Son, Jesus, to the world to offer us a special gift.

Connect the dots to see the picture.

© 2014 Warner Press, Inc All rights reserved

Jesus grew up in a town called Nazareth.

Find and circle these objects hidden in the picture:
ball, hammer, fish, cross, Bible

© 2014 Warner Press, Inc All rights reserved

Every year His parents took a trip to Jerusalem for the Feast of the Passover.

Help Jesus and His family reach Jerusalem.

© 2014 Warner Press, Inc All rights reserved

When Jesus was 12 years old, the family went to Jerusalem as always. But on the way home Jesus' parents couldn't find Him anywhere. Where was He?

Color in all the spaces with dots to find out.

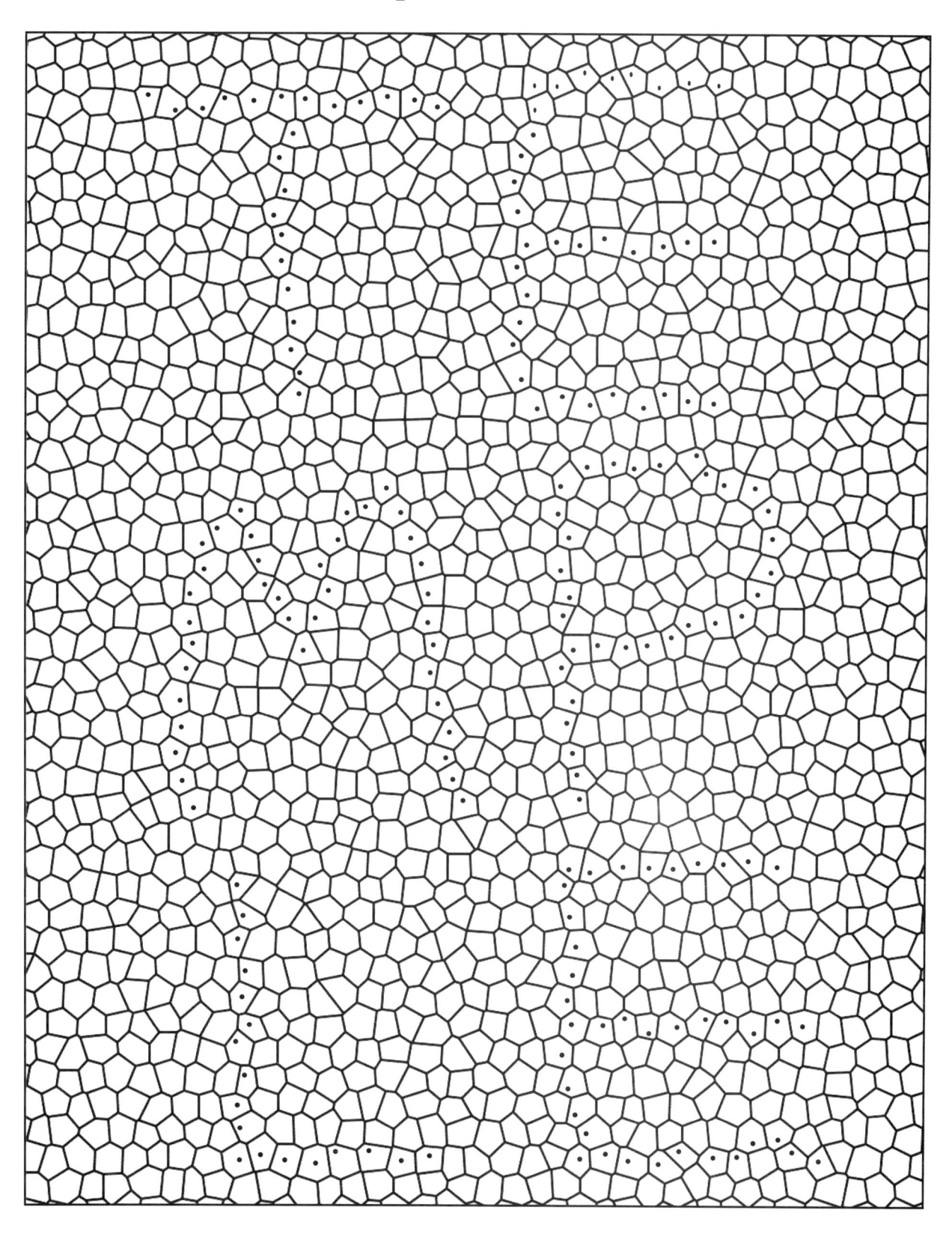

© 2014 Warner Press, Inc All rights reserved

The teachers were amazed at all that Jesus knew about God.
Jesus knew that God had a special job
for Him to do when He grew up.

Circle 5 things that do not belong in the picture.

© 2014 Warner Press, Inc All rights reserved

Jesus wanted to be baptized before He began His work. When Jesus came up from the water, God sent down His spirit in the form of a dove. What did God say?

Use the code to fill in the blanks and read the message.

___ ___ ___   ___ ___ ___
13   8   11   1   22   3

___ ___   ___ ___ ___,
7   13   10 8   20

___ ___ ___ ___   ___
12 17 8   7   5

___ ___ ___ ___;   ___ ___ ___ ___
19 8   24 3   12 5   23 17

___ ___ ___   ___
13 8   11   5

___ ___   ___ ___ ___ ___
1   7   12 3   19 19

___ ___ ___ ___ ___ ___ ___. Luke 3:22 (NIV1984)
21 19 3   1   10 3   15

CODE

A	B	C	D	E	F	G	H	I	J	K	L	M
1	14	2	15	3	16	4	17	5	18	6	19	7
N	O	P	Q	R	S	T	U	V	W	X	Y	Z
20	8	21	9	22	10	23	11	24	12	25	13	26

© 2014 Warner Press, Inc All rights reserved

Jesus chose 12 men called disciples to help with His work.
Which men did Jesus choose?

Solve the math problems.
If the answer is 12, color the disciple.

4 x 3

6 x 2

11 + 1

22 − 3

9 + 3

20 − 8

8 + 4

6 + 6

24 ÷ 2

5 x 3

15 − 3

12 x 1

2 + 10

9 + 7

7 + 5

© 2014 Warner Press, Inc All rights reserved

Unscramble the letters to read the names of the 12 disciples.

Hint: Read Matthew 10:2-4 (NIV1984) if you need help.

MOSIN TERPE   _____ _____

EWANDR   _____

AMEJS   _____

JHNO   _____

LIPPHI   _____

OLOTHMEWBAR   _____

TMASHO   _____

WTHMATE   _____

ESJAM, NSO FO PUSHAALE _____ _____ ___

                       _____

USTAEHADD   _____

MSINO ETH ALOTZE   _____ _____

                       _____

DAJUS ARCIOTIS   _____ _____

© 2014 Warner Press, Inc All rights reserved

Then Jesus began teaching people
about God and His great love for all of us.
And He taught us how we should love God,
Jesus and others.

Solve the crossword puzzle about love.

Across

1. "The reason my _____ loves me is that I lay down my life— only to take it up again." *(John 10:17)*

3. Jesus said, "Love your _____ and pray for those who persecute you." *(Matthew 5:44)*

5. "No servant can serve two _____. Either he will hate the one and love the other, or he will be devoted to the one and despise the other." *(Luke 16:13)*

7. "Love the Lord your God with all your _____ and with all your soul and with all your mind." *(Matthew 22:37)*

8. "By this all men will know that you are my _____, if you love one another." *(John 13:35)*

9. Love your _____ as yourself. *(Matthew 19:19)*

Down

1. Jesus said, "Greater love has no one than this, that he lay down his life for his _____." *(John 15:13)*

2. "If you love me, you will obey what I _____." *(John 14:15)*

4. "If you love those who love you, what credit is that to you? Even '_____' love those who love them." *(Luke 6:32)*

6. "Because of the increase of wickedness, the love of most will _____ _____." *(Matthew 24:12)*

Why did God send Jesus, His only Son, to earth?

Write the first letter of each picture.
Then read the verse to discover why Jesus came.

For □□□ □□ loved

the □□□□□ that □□

□□□□ □□□ □□□

and only □□□, that

whoever believes in □□□

shall not □□□□□□

but have eternal □□□□.

— John 3:16

The time had come for the Passover celebration, so Jesus and His disciples started toward Jerusalem. When they were close, Jesus told two of His disciples to go into the next village and find an animal for Him to ride.

Help the disciples find the next village.

Start

End

Many people who welcomed Jesus threw their robes down for His donkey to walk on.

Color in the underlined words above in the puzzle below. Then put the letters you did NOT color in the blanks below to find out what the people shouted to welcome Jesus.

__ __ __ __ __ __ __ __ __ !

Matthew 21:9

Jesus then went to a town called Bethany and stayed at the home of Simon the Leper. While He was there, a woman poured something special on Jesus' head. The disciples thought it was a big waste of money, but Jesus said she had done a beautiful thing for Him. What did the woman pour on Jesus? (John 12:2-8)

Cross out every Q, Z, and K.
Then write the letters you have left on the lines.

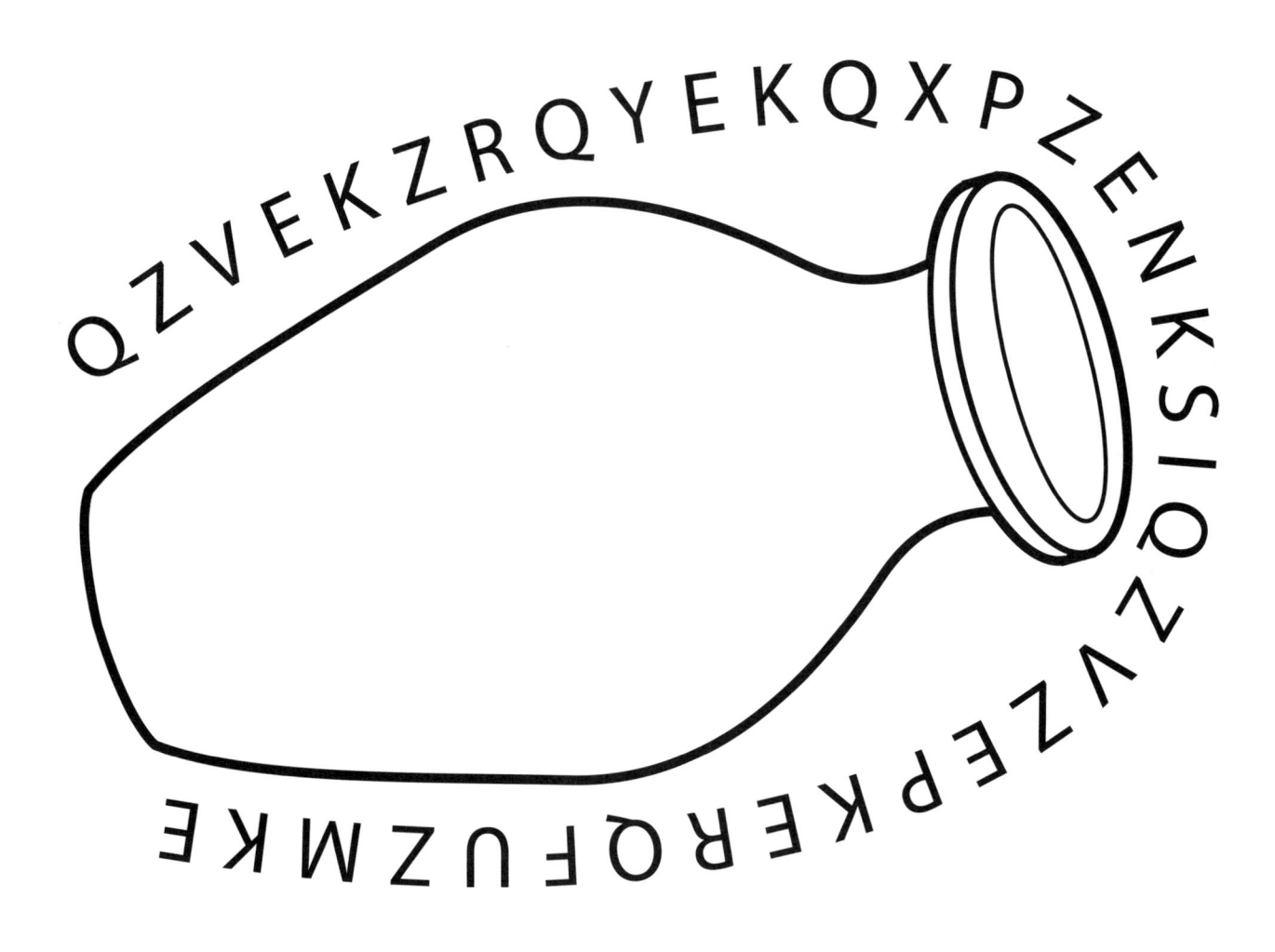

QZVEKZRQYEKQXPZENKSIOZYZQFEKPEZYZUMKE

___ ___ ___ ___ ___ ___ ___   ___ ___ ___ ___ ___ ___

___ ___ ___ ___ ___

Jesus and His disciples were going to eat a special meal together. What was it called?

Find all of the letters hidden in this picture. Then unscramble them and read the word.

__ __ __ __ __ __ __ __

As the evening meal was served, Jesus got up
from the table and wrapped a towel around His waist.
He took a bowl of water and began washing
His disciples' feet and drying them with the towel.
Why did Jesus do this?

Write the letter on the line that comes AFTER the letter
under the line. Then read the message.

___ ___ A ___ ___
 H   G   U   D

___ ___ ___   ___ ___ ___   A ___
 R   D   S   X   N   T   M

___ ___ A ___ ___ ___ ___
 D   W   L   O   K   D

___ ___ A ___   ___ ___ ___
 S   G   S   X   N   T

___ ___ ___ ___ ___ ___   ___ ___
 R   G   N   T   K   C   C   N

A ___   ___   ___ A ___ ___
    R   H   G   U   D

___ ___ ___ ___   ___ ___ ___
 C   N   M   D   E   N   Q

___ ___ ___.   John 13:15 (NIV1984)
 X   N   T

A B C D E F G H I J K L M N O P Q R S T U V W X Y Z

© 2014 Warner Press, Inc All rights reserved

While they ate, Jesus told the disciples many things.
Then He shared bread and wine with them. "Whenever you
eat the bread and drink the wine, remember Me," Jesus said.

Draw a line between the points listed to draw
a surprise picture. The first line is done for you.

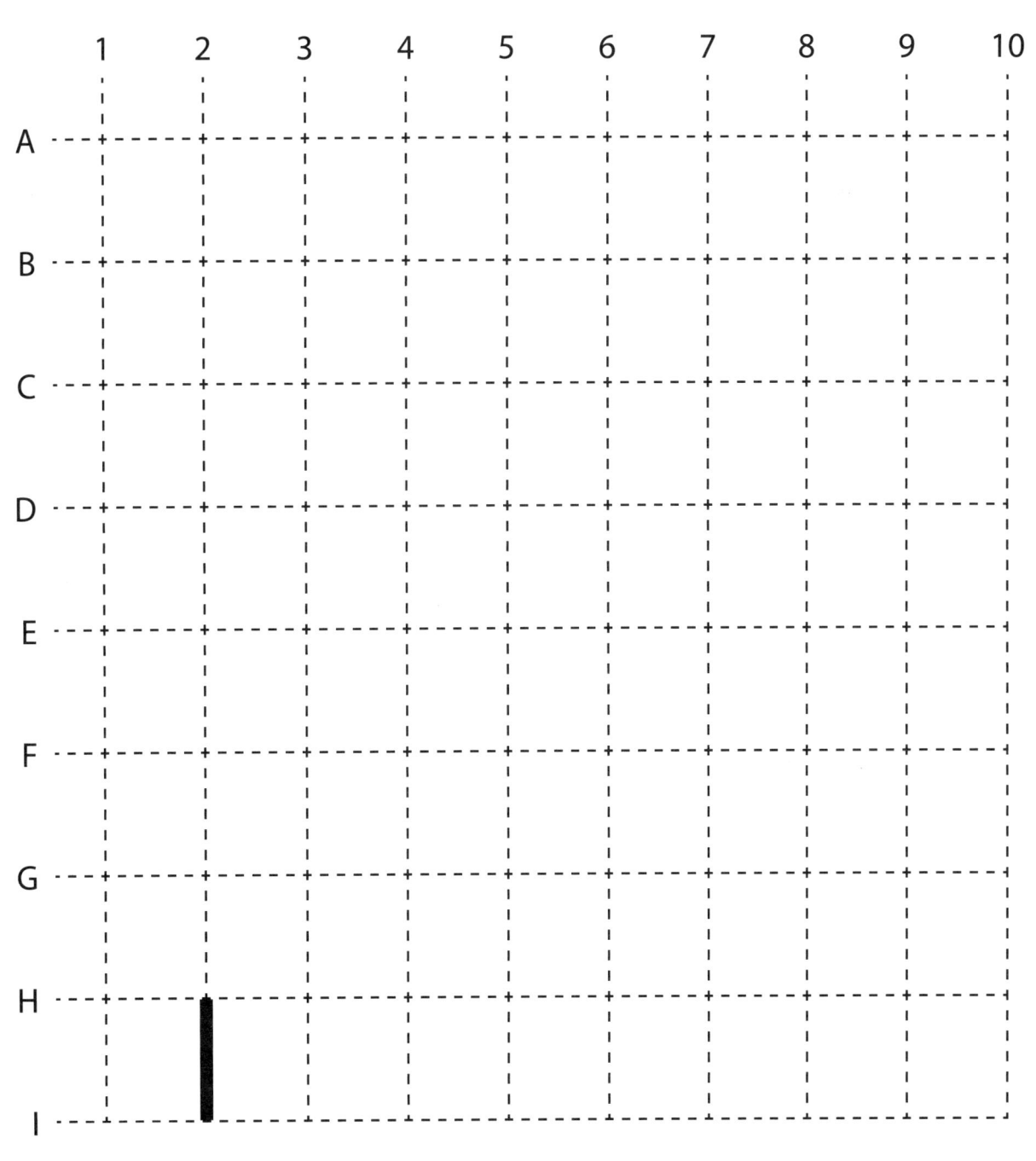

I2 – H2 – G1 – F1 – E2 – E3 – E4 – E5 –
F6 – G6 – H5 – I5 - I6 – I7 – H8 – G8 – F8 – E7 – D7 –
C7 – C8 – C9 – C10 – D10 – E10 – F9 – G9 – H9 – I10

© 2014 Warner Press, Inc All rights reserved

Jesus used the bread and wine as symbols to help us remember the sacrifice He was about to make on the cross. We now call these symbols by a special name. What is it?

Follow the letters through the maze, writing each letter on the blank below as you come to it. Then read the word.

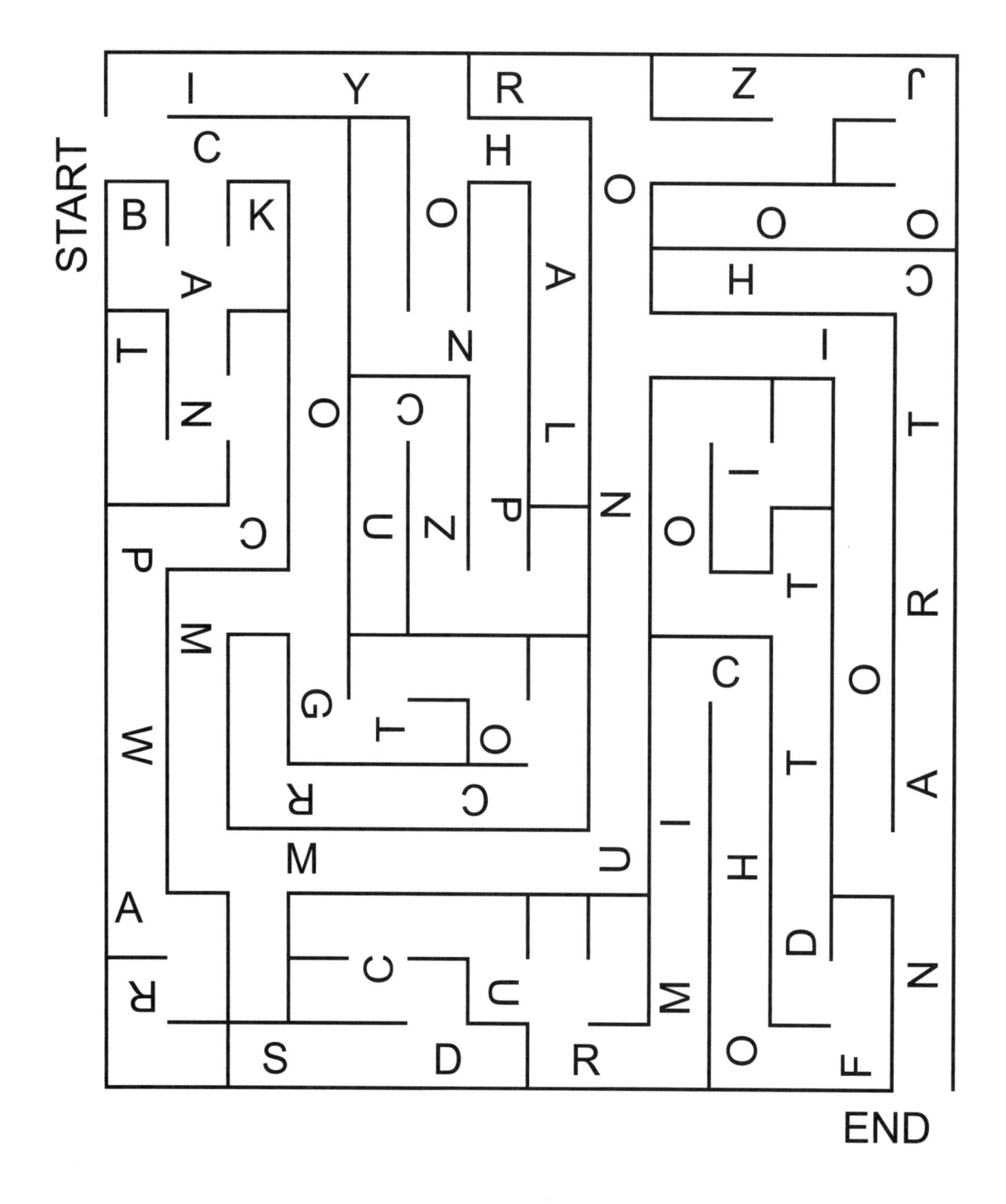

___ ___ ___ ___ ___ ___ ___ ___

After the meal, Jesus and His disciples went out to the Mount of Olives. Jesus told them that soon they would all leave Him, but Peter promised he never would. Jesus said that before a certain animal made a noise Peter would have denied Him three times.

What animal did Jesus mention?
Color by numbers to find out.

1 = brown   2 = red   3 = yellow

4 = black   5 = orange   6 = blue

© 2014 Warner Press, Inc All rights reserved

Jesus knew that soon He would be killed, and His heart was sad. What did Jesus pray?

Fit the letter blocks into the spaces.

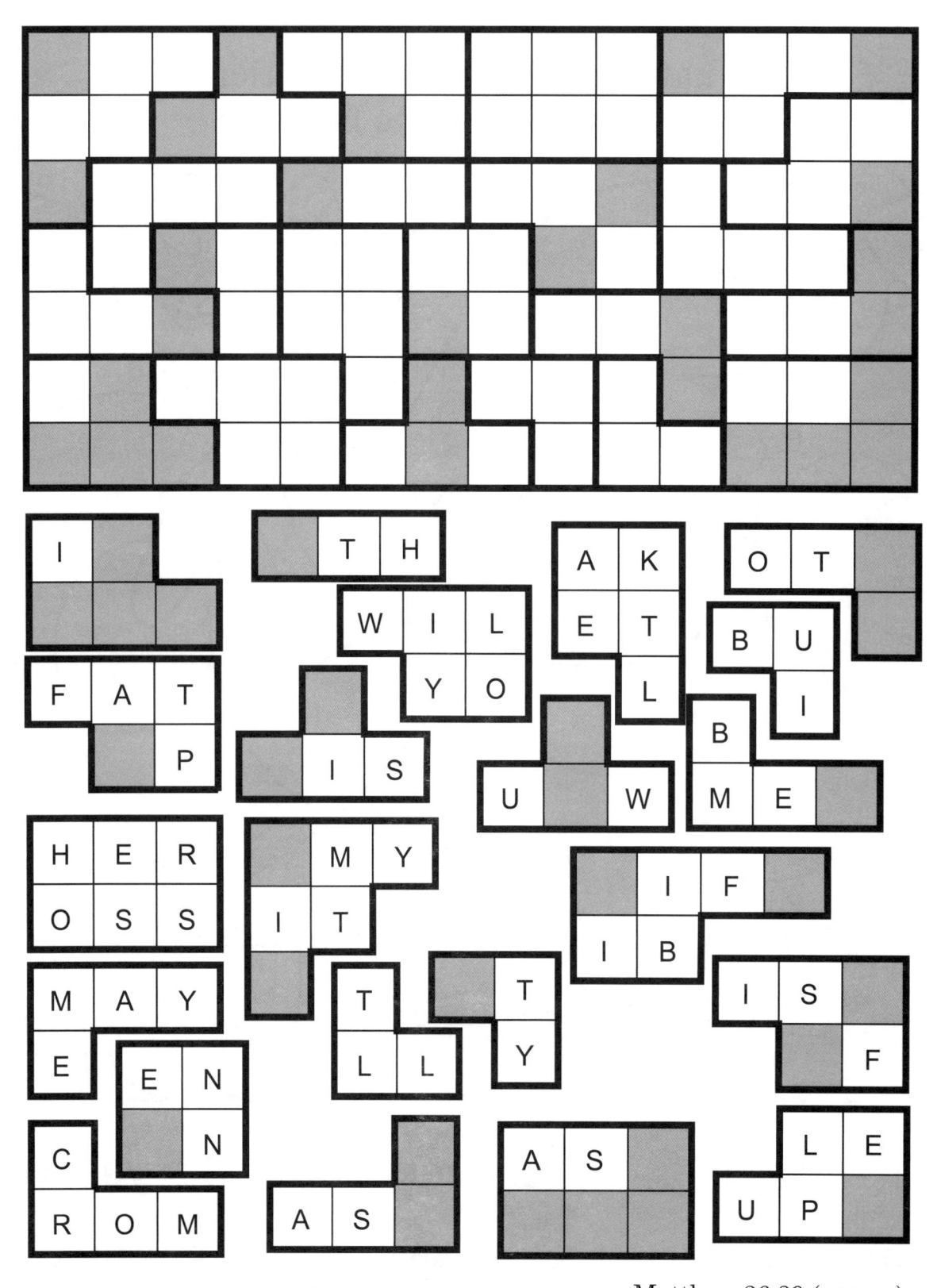

Matthew 26:39 (NIV1984)

Just as Jesus finished praying,
one of the disciples came to betray Him.
Who was it?

Look at the object, then decide which letter
is missing from the word next to it.
When you have filled in all the missing letters,
you will find the name of the disciple who betrayed Jesus.

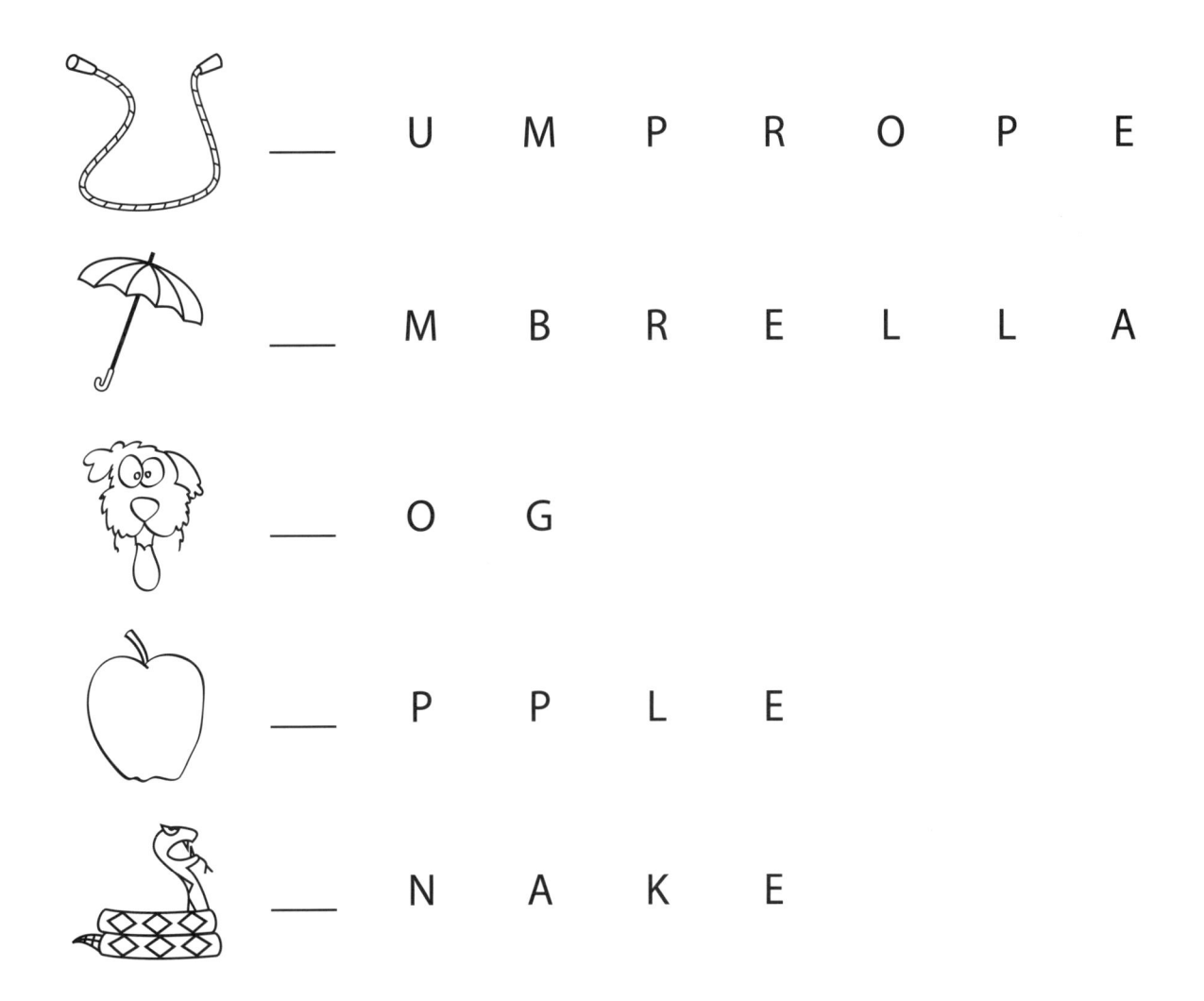

___ U M P R O P E

___ M B R E L L A

___ O G

___ P P L E

___ N A K E

___ ___ ___ ___ ___

© 2014 Warner Press, Inc All rights reserved

"What should I do with Jesus?" Pilate asked.
What did the people shout then?

Cross out every G, P, and Z. Then write the letters you have left on the lines and read the words.

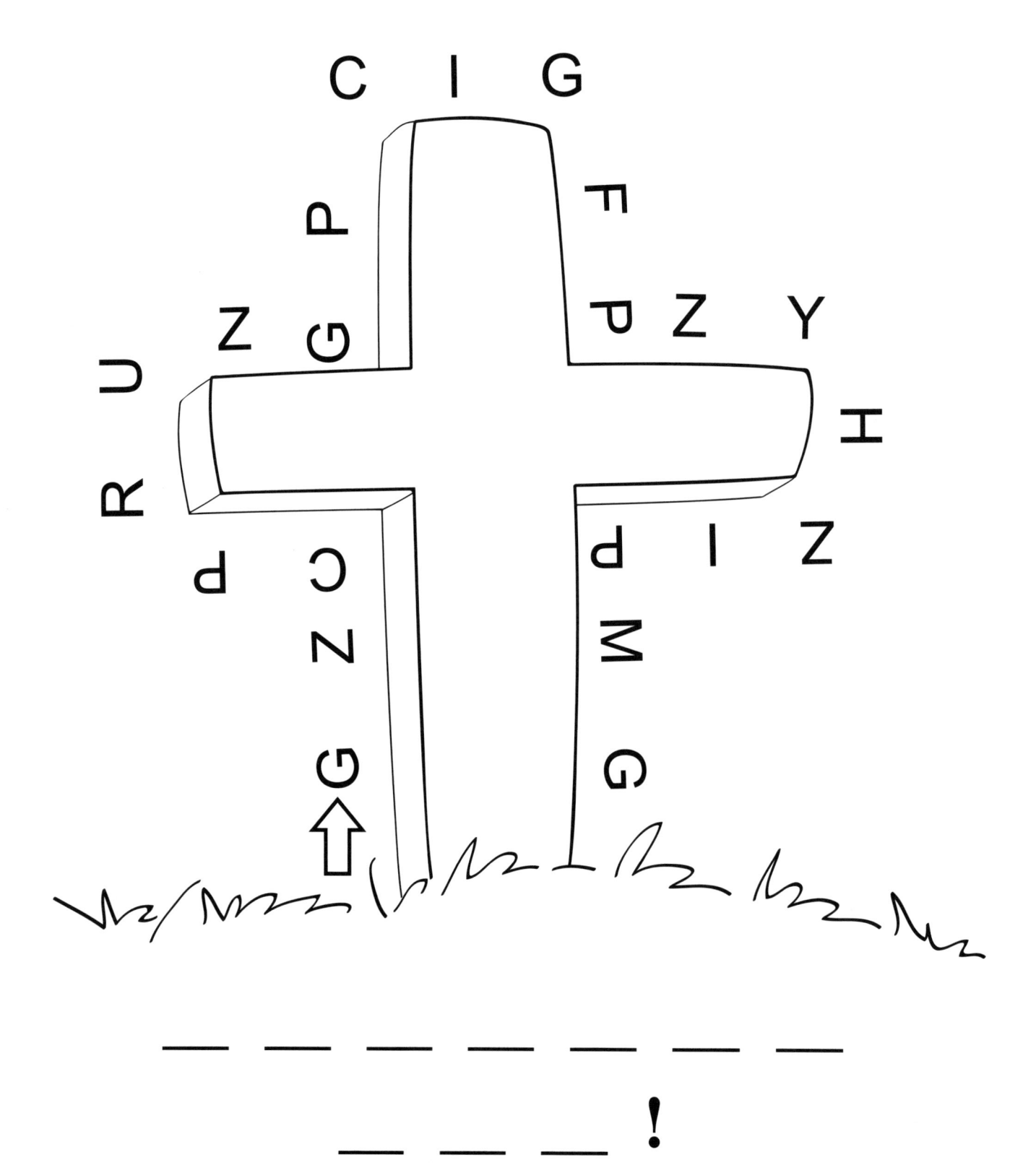

_ _ _ _ _ _ _

_ _ _ !

Soldiers took Jesus away.
They dressed Him like a king, made fun of Him and hit Him.
They put something on His head.
What was it?

Color in all the spaces with dots to see the picture.

© 2014 Warner Press, Inc All rights reserved

They made Jesus carry a heavy wooden cross to a place called Golgotha, which means "the place of the Skull." They nailed Him to a cross and placed it between the crosses of two thieves.

Color the shapes with dots in them to see a picture of the cross.

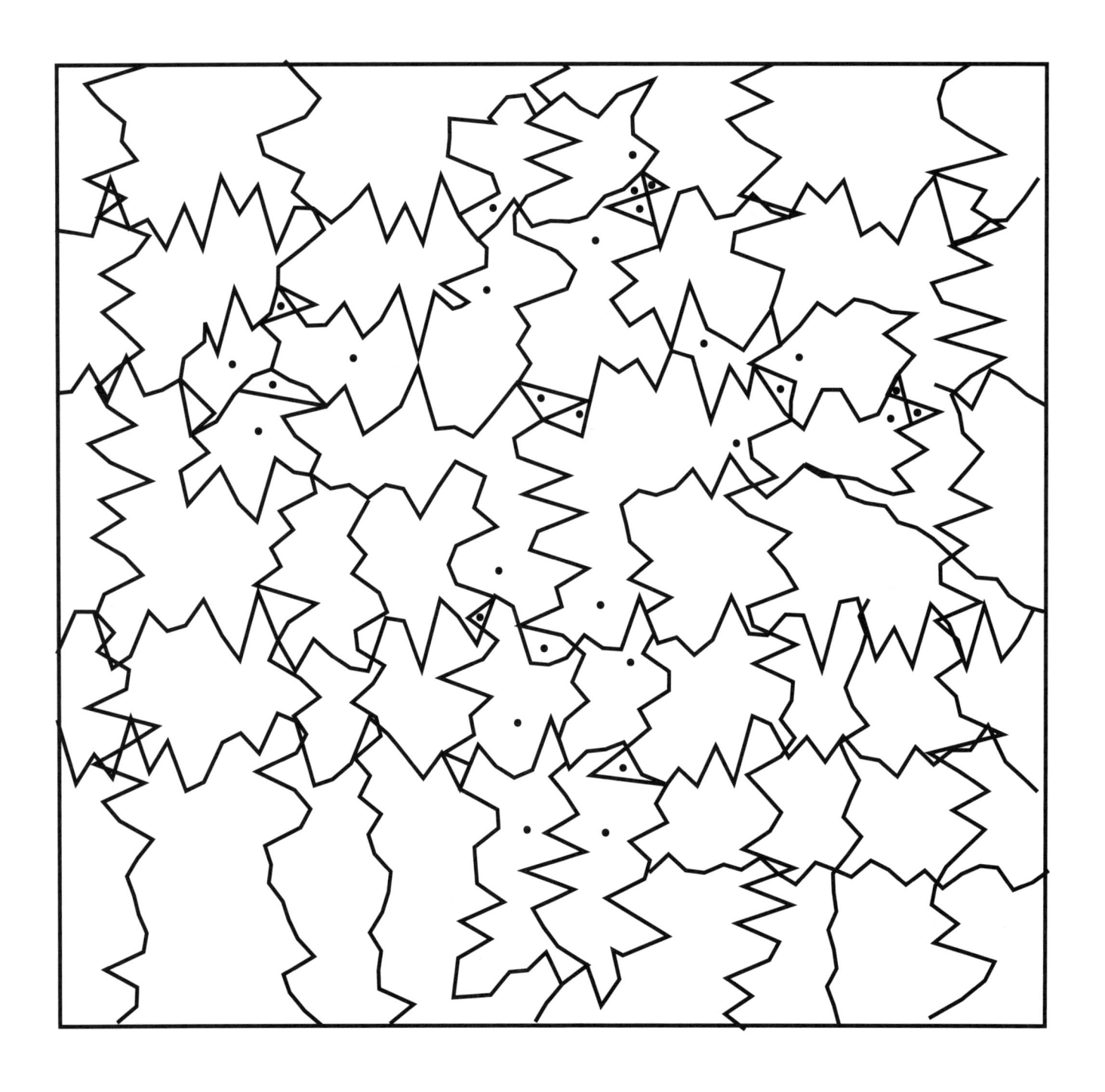

Jesus was nailed to a cross and placed between the crosses of two thieves.

Connect the dots to see the picture.

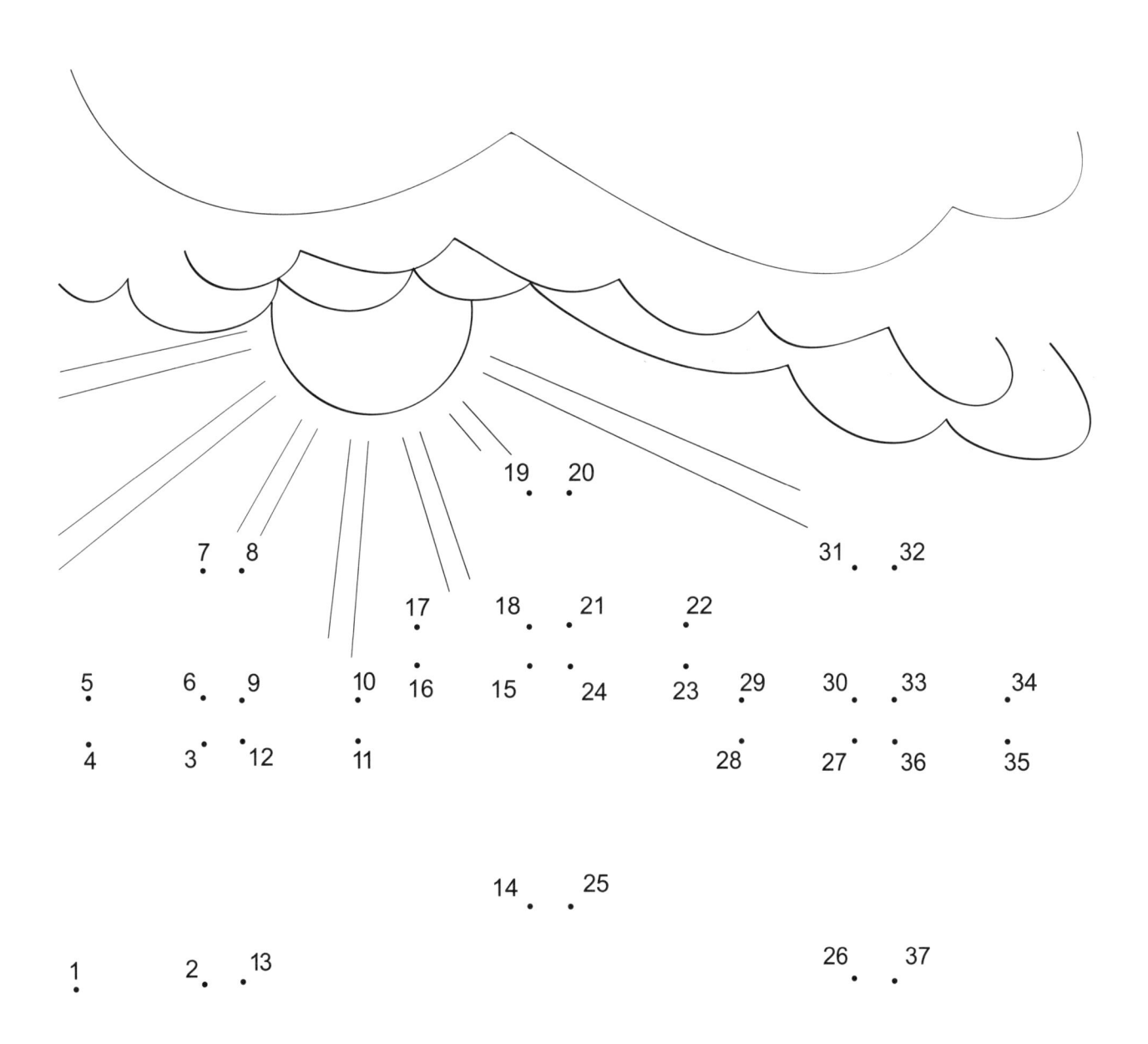

Pilate had a sign written and nailed to Jesus' cross. What did it say?

Use the secret code to read the message.

__J__ __E__ __S__ __U__ __S__   __O__ __F__
17 22   8   6   8   12 21

__N__ __A__ __Z__ __A__ __R__ __E__ __T__ __H__,
13 26   1   26   9   22   7   19

__T__ __H__ __E__   __K__ __I__ __N__ __G__
7   19   22   16   18   13   20

__O__ __F__   __T__ __H__ __E__
12   21   7   19   22

__J__ __E__ __W__ __S__
17 22   4   8

CODE

A	B	C	D	E	F	G	H	I	J	K	L	M
26	25	24	23	22	21	20	19	18	17	16	15	14
N	O	P	Q	R	S	T	U	V	W	X	Y	Z
13	12	11	10	9	8	7	6	5	4	3	2	1

© 2014 Warner Press, Inc All rights reserved

The sky grew dark. Finally, Jesus cried out in a loud voice and died. At that moment the curtain in the temple was torn in two, the earth shook and the rocks cracked apart. Tombs opened and many holy people came to life again.

Fit the words into the puzzle.

3 LETTERS	4 LETTERS	5 LETTERS	6 LETTERS	7 LETTERS
SKY	DARK	JESUS	MOMENT	CURTAIN
OUT	LOUD	CRIED	TEMPLE	
TWO	DIED	VOICE	PEOPLE	
	TORN	EARTH		
	HOLY	ROCKS		
	LIFE	TOMBS		

As evening came, a rich man named Joseph went to Pilate, asking if he could take Jesus' body, and Pilate said he could. Joseph wrapped Jesus' body in a clean linen cloth and laid it in his own new tomb. Then he rolled a big stone in front of the entrance.

Find five differences in the two pictures.

© 2014 Warner Press, Inc All rights reserved

Two of Jesus' friends came to the tomb.
The stone was rolled away! An angel spoke to them.
Then the women ran to tell the disciples.
What did the angel say?

Write the letter on the line that comes BEFORE the letter under the line. Then read the message.

__ __   __ __   __ __ __
I F   J T   O P U

__ __ __ __;   __ __
I F S F   I F

__ __ __   __ __ __ __.
I B T   S J T F O

Matthew 28:6

| A | B | C | D | E | F | G | H | I | J | K | L | M |
| N | O | P | Q | R | S | T | U | V | W | X | Y | Z |

© 2014 Warner Press, Inc All rights reserved

The disciples were afraid! They thought they had seen a ghost when Jesus appeared to them in a room when the door was shut. "Feel my hands and feet," the man told them. "I'm not a ghost! Don't you remember what I told you?"

What had Jesus told the disciples?

Start at the arrow and cross out every Z. Then fill in the blanks with the letters you DID NOT cross out.

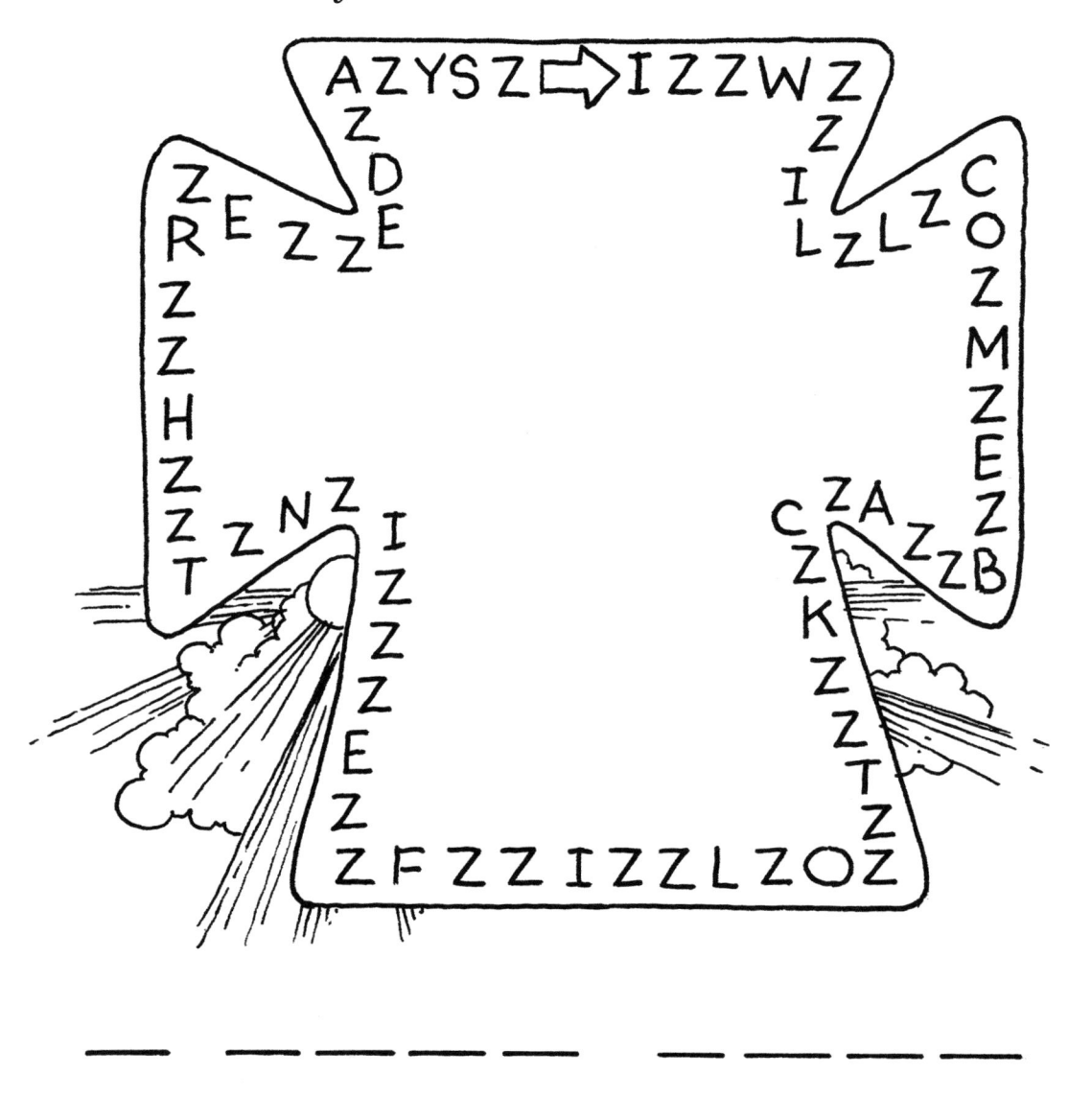

_ _ _ _ _ _ _ _ _

_ _ _ _ _ _ _ _ _

_ _ _ _ _ _ _ _ _ .

The Great Commission
from Matthew 28:19-20

Use the code chart to decode the special verse below.

CODE

A	B	C	D	E	F	G	H	I	J	K	L	M
✌	👌	👍	👎	👉	👈	☝	✋	🖐	🙂	😐	☹	💣

N	O	P	Q	R	S	T	U	V	W	X	Y	Z
♦	🏳	🏴	✈	☼	●	❄	✝	🔔	☦	✠	✡	☪

Go ye therefore, and teach all nations,

baptizing them in the name of the Father, and of the Son, and of the Holy Ghost:

Teaching them to observe all things whatsoever I have commanded you: and, lo, I am with you alway, even unto the end of the world.

Matthew 28:19-20 (KJV)

© 2014 Warner Press, Inc All rights reserved

Read the story in Acts 1:9-11; then find the words below.

LORD	SIGHT	DRESSED	TAKEN
TAKEN UP	LOOKING	WHITE	HEAVEN
EYES	INTENTLY	STOOD	COME
CLOUD	SKY	GALILEE	BACK
HID	TWO	STAND	SAME
HIM	MEN	JESUS	WAY

```
E H I D G C F Y X Z E B U T
E Z D L L E F E M O C U O A K
L I U C L O Z H M C W X K A S
I S O N O K R S E E L E A T E
L U L M O Q D D I A N P X U Y
A S C B K Q T E Z G V M I O E
G E H E I F D Y S P H E X Q S
T J I N N V L T C S B T N E T
I A M N G T E N D E E K J R A
B Z R K N B D N A T S R F T K
A R T E D V Y A W Y T B D M E
C J T U D W Q S A K O X T Z N
K N N S L A Y Q A S O W T T U
I A Q F E K I P Q M D C E V P
D I Q M S H W H I T E Z B Q J
```

© 2014 Warner Press, Inc All rights reserved